MW00917039

Ignite Your Light

Anu Arora

Copyright © 2018 Anu Arora

All rights reserved. This book or any portion thereof
may not be reproduced or used in any manner whatsoever
without the express written permission of the author
except for the use of brief quotations in a book review. For
permission requests, send email to the author at
anu@infinitepotentialleadership.com

DEDICATION

In the space where the boundaries cease

Just the energies exist

Everything is sensed and felt

You met me there

I dedicate this to you

Anu Arora

A collection of daily affirmations in short poems!

A few years ago, I started the practice of journaling daily, mostly writing my intentions for the day and sometimes what I was experiencing in the moment. Initially, it felt good to write but as time went by, the intentions started to manifest. This was both powerful and transformational.

I wrote my intentions to be aligned with who I wanted to be. Sometimes, I wrote to get inspired and motivated. On other days, it was to gather courage for a tough conversation.

My muse is inspired by nature, life around me and the books I am reading at the time.

Anu Arora

CONTENTS

	Acknowledgments	11
1	Courage	13
2	Love	31
3	Happiness	39
4	Inspiration	47
5	Living in the moment	63
6	Acceptance	83
7	Celebration	95

AN INVITATION

Dear Friends,

I decided to write this book as I felt that this was the best way, I could share with you the simple shifts that have helped me create a new life for myself. A life which is expanded and enriched with joy, beauty and happiness.

For the last decade I have been studying on what makes us happy. I constantly seek ways that move us towards the positive. What was surprising is, how much of what happens in our life is within our control.

My invitation for you is to read this book with an intention. An intention that this book brings you insights, to create the life you want.

My hope is that this book ignites your inner light and helps you explore your own infinite potential.

Please share your experiences with me at:
anu@infinitepotentialleadership.com.

Love and Light
Anu

x

ACKNOWLEDGMENTS

My coach Sophie Bizeul who encouraged me to free my fearless soul. Sophie, this is the way I chose to do it.

Sharmin Banu, the President of International Coach Federation's Washington Chapter (an organization I currently serve), who is my mentor and friend. She doesn't hesitate to give me honest feedback.

My friend Mamta Hathi, whose unflagging support on whatever I choose to do, has become a pillar of strength for me.

My sons, Ranjan and Julian, who, are my source of joy. Their smiles light up my heart.

Pradeep, my partner in love for over 30 years and counting. He has enthusiastically supported me in all my projects, giving me invaluable insights.

Anu Arora

Courage

This one ingredient in my life has made all the difference. I have to constantly remind myself to be courageous. Some days, it still escapes me. The days I find it, I dance with the universe. We become one.

The Choice Is Ours

To be conquered by fear
Or conquer that fear
The choice is ours

To be defeated by others
Or to defeat their attempts
To defeat us
The choice is ours

To be led by others or lead ourselves
The choice is ours

I have made a choice to lead myself
Let's see where it leads to

The Power Of Reset

Every once in a while, the computer gets stuck
Just freezes
For many reasons
Out of memory?
or meets a conflict?
or is overloaded with scrambled data?
All resources are maximized
way over the limit
And then there is the power of reset

A fresh start
Clears all memory
Devices get initialized once again
To a new beginning

Every once in a while
Our lives seem that way
Overwhelmed and crazy
Running in many directions
Mind and body exhausted and maximized

Remember the reset!
A fresh start
To release the past
And wake up with a new smile
The power of letting go
Is greater then
The power of holding on!

Capture The Day

I capture you today
Not like a warrior
Or a soldier
With any weapons

I capture you today
Not like a lover
Or a professor
Suffocating you
with obsessive attention

I capture you today
Like a giver
I give all of me to you
I capture you today

Life

Life is too short to play small
Big in heart
Big in action
Big to forgive
Big to move on
Big in love

Let's live this life
On the big screen

Without a worry
Without a doubt

With the heart singing songs
And actions worthwhile

For Every Worry Under The Sun

For every worry under the sun
There may be a way out
Or perhaps there is none

If there is one
Let's find out
If there is none
Never mind!

Let's stop fighting
Every worry under the sun

A Prayer

A prayer on my lips
To make today shine

I am back with my experiment
Of being happy and alive

To shoo the fears
Which come in the way

To not get stuck
When it gets tough

See life as a game
A puzzle to solve

Some days, it will be fun to solve
On others, it will not resolve

A Year Of Light

This is a year of Light
I experiment
With curiosity,
Innocence
and
A fearless soul

There is no more fight, freeze or flight
My projects are deliberate
I use the lever principle
To propel
I use all my time on earth
And before
To move to the next

I don't reinvent
What's been done
I experiment
To create new

The universe complies
As if it was waiting all the time
For me to be me!

I Do It

I commit
I do it

Everyday a little bit
Every single day

It is with grit
Building it up bit by bit

Till it becomes true
The castle is ready
For me to live in

The stars shine
Everything aligns

I feel one with the universe
There is no confusion

Until then bit by bit
I do it

Yes

Yes, to a big change
To a growth phase
A brand-new challenge
Somewhat scared, a little excited
As I dare to imagine it
It becomes possible
It opens up the world
To allow me to live
And let my fearless soul be free

Do You Have The Guts?

A life which has meaning
A life of grace
In the unexpected
A life full of joy
A life fulfilled
Is it too much to ask for?
Is it too much to ask of me?
Do I have the guts to be extraordinary?

I Rise Again

It has been a month
Since I died
I am ready to rise again
From my own ashes
Lifting my dead spirit
Filling it with life and hope
With vigor and zeal
With head and heart
With a thought, feeling and intellect
With a new learning
That every moment is precious

With a new resolve
I rise again

Find My Dream

Climbing the mountains
Zipping the ziplines
I even went on a dogsled
to find my dream

Exploring the new
Listening to my soul
On what it wants me do
Then courageously taking the plunge
Committing to something small
Meaningful and joyful

Until I find it
I know, I will my dream

I Ride Again

Paranoia grips me
Fear cripples me
My neck reminds me
My heart questions me
The cracked blue helmet mocks at the new gray one
'You will ride with her?'
And, then I hear a voice
'Anu, where are you?'
Here I am!
Paddling away
Slowly and steadily
Ok, not laughing or flying yet
I am back on the bike again
The neck, shoulders and heart have no chance
The new helmet looks down and says
'I am with you'
Glad you are!
Glad you are!

Shake It Off

Shake it off
Like a wet dog
A big hearty shake

Take it all off
What it is holding you today?

Shake it off

Be in the flow
Finds reasons to smile
Go that extra mile
Love life with it its twists
Through the unknown, comes new gifts

Shake it off

Don't lose momentum
Trust that dreams manifest
Only if they get some air
They will breathe and come alive
For that you must rise

Even if it is a small step at a time
With every passing moment
Gets me closer to the dream realized

The Shit Hits The Fan

The shit hits the fan
All I hear is complain and threat

The first reaction is to resist
You have got it wrong, I insist

That sucks life out of me
With life force gone, I am a dead meat

She senses the tension, she gets back in action
She sees the weakness, comes right at me

I see myself a mess
Anger, frustration, a sudden tightness in the chest

I have hit a new low
That is not what I had sowed

My years of training a waste
Being aligned with the soul
Was always my goal

I remind myself of the resolve
And feel the resistance dissipate

First I connect with my breath
I am back as energy and spirit

Intention is back at play
I ask her to lead the way
I no longer resist
I let her take it out

After all is out, she is calm
We are past the storm

Together, we create
Something beautiful,
Which will manifest
We are well past detest

Anu Arora

Love

Love comes in various shapes and forms. Sometimes it is in a hug, other times it is the food my friend cooks and brings over when I am recovering from a fall. Love is essential for existence. Without love, nothing exists.

A Healing Touch

Sometimes all you need
Is a healing touch
And you can sleep again

Sometimes all you need
Is a tight hug
And the life is bright again

Sometimes you need
A kick in the butt
And you rise again

Sometimes you need
To be silly
The tender heart feels light again

Love

I love to see my love
Who I love so much

What measures love
The tears which roll down my face
The hug which won't let him go

Or the prayers for his wellness
The one who I love so much

Or, love is in letting go
Love has no discord

The universe will look after him
I need to believe in my prayer

And believe in my love for him

Somebody Is There For You

The plants in my room
Greener than green
Always there with me
Whether I am asleep or awake

Some even defy their natural rhythm
And flower in winter

Jasmine flowers are blooming now
They love to blossom
As they are not alone
There is someone
To wish them good morning
And good night

Sometimes just that is enough
That you are there for someone

Day of Love

We need a day of love
To remind us
That life is beautiful

For we are caught in what is wrong
A day when the world is
Not cruel, unjust or a sad song
Every emotion replaced by love
Every action based on it
To show us it is not all bad
We need a day of love

To love ourselves a little more
To allow ourselves to feel rich
With positivity, happiness and joy to the core
Today is the day of love

Love to care and care to love
Let it be just that
Tomorrow will be there, to tell you
What all is so bad.

For now, just soak in the day of love
Today is the day of love
Happy Valentines Day everyone

I Love You

I look in the mirror

Who is she?
I like her
She smiles at me
And says, 'I like you too'

I look at her again
And wonder,
'What if she can…'
She chides,
'Really, that's all what you care'
And disarms me with her smile

I notice her laugh lines
They are deeper than before

The crinkles around her eyes
Are well defined too

The gray in her hair
Is more than yesterday

Yet her curiosity about the world intact
She feels alive through the mirror

Resistance melts
She is perfect as she is
In this moment,
Creative and divine

I feel the power through her

She is happy
She whispers, 'I love you'.
I have no qualms to admit
That I love her too.

Anu Arora

Happiness

Happiness is not a constant. It is a source of my biggest mystery. I seek it with a passion. I am always striving towards it. What gives it? How do I bring more of that in my life and the life around me.

Happiness

Happiness is not an it
Happiness is not in things
Happiness is a deliberate effort
To make your inner light shine
Sometimes it is in inaction
Being still
Closing eyes
Connecting to the breath
Inhaling happiness
Exhaling obstructions
Today my happiness,
Is not an it!

Today, it is in my inhales and exhales
In those momentary pauses in between

I Decide To Smile Today

During the hike
I smiled at the sun-kissed hills
And they smiled back at me

I smiled at the knee-high golden grass
And it slightly brushed against me

I smiled at a father and son team
They wished me 'good morning'
With a generous laugh

Everything I smiled at
Smiled back at me

Another World

Beyond good and bad
Beyond happy and sad
Beyond love and hate

Another world exists
I invite you to there

It doesn't judge
It doesn't fret
It is just there

It is not dead
Very much alive
Sensing and feeling
Taking the unknown with a curiosity

It sings songs
It was born to sing

It doesn't shut off at the slight pretext
It creates new, without a fear
It connects to its source, like a seer

It doesn't compare
Self to others

It doesn't compare
Self to self

Any path is possible
Even the ones which don't exist

In flow, harmony and alignment
Another world exists

It is not passive
It is not compliant
It is disruptive
But doesn't resist
Another world exists

You Calm My Soul

Whenever I think of you
A smile comes to my lips

Enough to make my day bright
Everything around me perfectly alright

Compassion and wisdom beyond your years
Heart so kind, it brings me tears

With your jokes, you are on a roll
Your voice can calm my soul

You remind me every day
How to live in a grand and generous way

Happy For No Reason

I am happy
I don't know why

I smile a lot
For that feels right

I think of my sanctuary
I feel myself there

It has the beauty
And abundance
Which you can't find anywhere else
I feel happy

I look around me
And am filled with gratitude

I am happy
I don't know why

I feel like a miracle
I am a source of joy

Anu Arora

Inspiration

I want to be inspired and inspire others. We have such a short time on earth that we can't lose it in feeling defeated and uninspired. Some days I write to inspire myself.

There is a verse in ancient texts in Sanskrit, which has been a source of my biggest inspiration. It goes like this:

Om Purnamadah Purnamidam Purnat
  Purnamudachyate
Purnasya Purnamadaya Purnamevavashisyate

It means that everything is infinite. Each one of us is complete and whole is all respects. If you take the whole away from the whole, the whole still remains.

Who Am I?

I like to question
Who am I?

I don't always
Have an answer

This answer is worth every pound
It is not entangled in any doubt

I am an indomitable spirit

The universe made me that way
Complete and whole in everyway
I am a creation myself
Part of larger universe
In which I exist
In complete harmony and alignment with it

Each one of us, complete in every way
Filled with unfathomable wisdom

Complete alone and complete together
Each one of us a shining light

All, when all the lights combine
The universe has a reason to rejoice
Each spirit has found its voice

My work is very simple
Be present, aware
And don't resist

When I am in flow
I am connected to myself, the source and each one of
you.
I am complete in every respect

Jumping High

I jumped in joy
I jumped so high
I felt as if I touched the sky

I cried a few
The kind of tears
Which feel good to shed

Anything is possible
If you set your sights on it
I couldn't get over the fact
That it was happening right in front of me

Wake Up

I must wake up
Before it is too late

I must trust that the words will ring
To the song I was meant to sing

It could be a slight whisper
At the onset of the day

It could be in the sign I see
On the road which is marked for me

It could be in the rainbow in the sky
It could be in the tweet of the bird soaring high

I must wake up
Before it is too late

Pearls Necklace

I have collected pearls
Unique pearls
Different sizes and colors
Some rare some not
Each one precious
Distinctly me and mine
They make a necklace
One of a kind
It is called 'me'.

I Can Fly

It is pretty simple
I learnt it in my first year of engineering
The theory of flight
Reduce the drag
Increase the thrust
Use the wings to lift
Get lighter on your feet
It is that simple
The theory of flight

The pressure differential is all you need to get
Pressure to lift you up
Should be higher than the one which pulls you down
You have to run really hard to take off
To get past the resistance which can increase the drag

It is simple
The reality of flight
The trick is to try, try, try
Until I can fly!

A New Day

A new day is here
Still hazy, not clear
The ash in the sky
Smoke far and near

Yet the day is here
It didn't say
It doesn't feel good
I am not coming out
Let there be another night

It is out
For it knows
It has just one chance
To make its mark
And many of us waiting for this day
To go after their dreams
And make them come true

Exhilarated And Inspired

This requires courage
This requires discipline
As simple as that
Courage and discipline

We overcomplicate life
It is mostly simple

With just these two
Slowly but surely
I will get it done
Step by step
With one at a time
I will be at the end

I am not overwhelmed
I am exhilarated and inspired

I am confident
In my pursuit
I commit to it
With my heart and soul

I am exhilarated and inspired

The Voice Of Truth

Guided by Intuition
Fueled by the fire within my belly
Connected by the compassion within my heart

Stable through the emotional turmoil
Rooted and grounded to mother Earth

Blessed by the divine

May such be the quality of words
Which come out of my mouth, today!

Is This Heaven?

I feel loved
There is no angst
The body flows
The face glows
The heart is alive
The spirit of mine
Is connected to the divine

I am in harmony with the universe
It must be heaven

I have reasons to smile
I am energized
The light is radiating all around me
I am in heaven

I Yearn To Learn

I yearn to learn
From teachers
From the subtleties
The intricacies
The practicalities
Of life

What the books don't teach
What is not on the world wide web
What is just felt and sensed
What is just in the moment

I salute all my teachers who taught
What I yearn to learn

Expire By Date

I have an expire by date
You have it too

I get the impermanence
Our spirit has to go
I don't know where

I am here
Just for few days

Could I make it more meaningful?
From one human to another
From one breath to another

When you remember me
Perhaps you can say
She lived with an open heart
And a smile

Monday

I embrace Monday
With a smile
And it smiles at me
I brush off the weird dream
of a stressed beginning of the day
And it creates a new one

Bright and beautiful
I smell the spring
It ignites my light

The new seeds are germinating
To become something real today

The Root Connection

I walk on this Earth
I feel connected to it
To my roots
Rock solid
Connected to my family, friends, my heritage, my
ancestors

I walk on this earth
I feel connected to the sun
I look into its eyes
I whisper 'thank you'
I look at it again
Can't meet its eyes
It is brighter
Says 'got it'
I have to shine brighter
Too many people saying 'thank you'

I take my shoes off
Bare feet on the dew pearls lying on the grass
I feel the grass
I smell the scent of grass and dew
I am grateful for all that I have got

Are You Yesterday?

No, you are not yesterday
I am sure!

The birds are singing a different song
They have new guests
It is a new dawn

I have a small stone by my bedside
Engraved with words
'With your thoughts you make the world'
It makes me smile

What thoughts will I entertain
What will make my today

Can it be thought of love and joy?
Can I make my today better than yesterday?

The Weight Lifts

There is sigh of relief
As the weight lifts
From the heart

Not as difficult as I thought

I suffered
Because I let myself
Be caught in the draught

There is plenty for me
Abundance in fact
No reason for me
To be distraught

Believing in the laws of attraction
I pray that I only attract what feeds my soul
Takes me away from the devious game of thought

Our biggest war is with us
The weight lifts
A fearless soul cannot be bought

Living in the moment

When I am in my head, I lose being in the moment. When I am obsessively checking my phone, I lose being in the moment. When I am reacting, I lose being in the moment. I am deliberate in my attempt to be present. Not always successful, but always trying.

Luxury Of Time

Stunning in bright yellow jacket
That it hurts the eye
Gregarious and brave
I am mesmerized

The gold finch on my birdfeeder
Patiently takes out
One seed at a time

Removing and discarding the skin
Devouring and relishing every bite

It is in no hurry to fly
Breakfast is being served
And we both have luxury of time

Beauty Of Autumn

The beauty of autumn
Is coming through my window
The maples are changing color
One leaf at a time
I snooze for 15 minutes
And there are more leaves
Which have turned
Orange, red and brown
Moments are passing away
Life is going by
I must wake up
To witness
The beauty of autumn
Which is passing by

Ignite My light

The air is still
Everything has stopped

The room is quiet
But for the clock
Goes tick-tock tick-tock

Thoughts run wild
They fill up the room
Still don't rest
They run out
Sweeping the still air

I ask them why they work so hard
Why don't they stop
So that we create the present

I don't know what clicks
They change their mind
Together we, ignite my light

A Door Opens

A door opens slightly
It is enough for just a ray
To get in
And fill up the entire
Room with brightness

It is our light which frightens us

It our brightness which blinds us
Our light which frightens us
Our fearlessness which scares us
Our limitlessness which limits us
Our strength which weakens us

I will not let myself come in my own way

Stellar Jay

On my deck
With a taunting look
It said to me
'It is a gold finch you adore,
My blueness you ignore'.

How can I?
You are so royally blue.
With prominent crest and gray hues

I hear you are intelligent
I am here for you

If I can love her
I can love you too

I hope you visit again
You flew away too soon

Reliving Moments With Old Friends

Uncontrollable laughter
crazy humor
Sharing the secrets
Only we knew

Of the days
When the spirits ran wild
The air was filled of mystery
Everything an experiment

The crazy, silly and weird times
Who knew in the future
Will be the moments we will treasure

Friends is all what mattered
Is what was so clear then

Friends is all what matters
Is understood once again

Awake

At dawn, I am up and awake
I welcome the new day with curiosity
Of what it might bring
Rain or Shine
Easy or Hard
New experiences
Are what matters
For there will be no growth
If each day was the same as before
It will be like the groundhog kind of way

Paradise

In search of my path
I found a paradise
In my backyard

I dare a honeybee to stay on the flower
The honeybee dared me by coming right at me

I watch the butterflies white and red
Hanging on to the dear roses with so much unrest
I try to catch one
She is faster than me
And off goes on a different quest

I chase a rabbit on the trail
Where blackberries grow wild
I eat berries to my heart's desire
While the poor rabbit hides inside

Conversations

Everything happens
Through conversations
The ones I am having in my head
In my heart
And with you!

Oops, they are all different
Causes pain and confusion

Let's make it one
The conversations are aligned
What a relief!

Come Out And Dance

On a bright winter morning
I look out of my window

I see the bare branches of the maples
Carrying the sun with pride
Beaming with light

Through the new space in-between
My eyes reach the trail
The sun is visiting the river too
Sitting majestically on its surface

And nearby, the squirrel is dancing on the branches
Sending me an invite
Why are you sitting in the quilt?
Come out and dance
You don't want to carry the guilt
Of missing my celebration
In your hours of deliberation
Come out and dance

Prayer

This must be my personal shrine
I ache to be here
I feel your energy through me
I know my trip will be incomplete
If I was not at your shrine

You are here with me
I pray in your compound
I don't know the customs
I don't even know what to say
I don't know how many times I should bow
and how many incense sticks to burn
I just want to be here
In your embrace

This is the moment
This is the moment when everything ceases
It is just you and me
I hear your benediction
In this moment
I was meant to be here
this was meant to be!

Together

Vapor trails on a mixed kind of day
With some sun and some clouds at play

Drawing lines all over the sky
Nature and technology dancing together

For a moment, it is difficult
To tell, if it is the clouds
Or the trail of the plane, just gone by

Am I Free?

A slow and typical Sunday
Warms up by afternoon
The trails are empty
The city is caught in the
Frenzy of the football game
I am free

Or am I?
I am caught in the work
Which needs to get done
The list I need to get caught up on
Always cracking the whip on myself
Am I really free?

No One Knows

The complex nature of our hearts
What do we think?
What do we feel?
What do we see?
What do we hear?
No one knows
Sometimes we don't know it too
Only if we can be
Right here, with us
Present in every sense of the way
Perhaps, we may see us
We will hear our words
And we will fall in love with ourselves
With the beauty of our souls

Tomorrow

Tomorrow I will wake again
Right at dawn
Open my drapes
See the drapes of greenery
Welcoming me into the new day
The birds tweeting a new song
For now, I sleep and rest
To prepare me the best
The body, mind and soul refreshed
To make tomorrow worth
Its weight in gold
I rest!

The Hidden World

Everything we see
Hides something else

And we always want to see
What is hidden by what we can see

Standing in front of the mirror
I don't see myself
How can that be?

My world is not yours
Your's not mine

Today my attention is
On what I can't see

Central Park In Spring

The leafless elms found their leaves
They look fashionable in the new green

The cherry blossoms shed their petals
Turning the earth below them into a
White and pink carpet

Tiny five petaled white flowers
With heads which are pink
Perhaps millions on those Hawthorn trees

Magnolias are not far behind
Many blooming ones you find

Winds are inspired by the museum of art nearby
Playing like an artist of modern times
Blows hard and soft to bring
Burst of color to the ground
Or sometimes design a flowers mound

Spring is at its best
In the city of New York's central park

Madame, You Must Die

I try to remember the dream
Which woke me up at three

First I remember the words so harsh,
It was about my last call on Earth

Then I remember the details
Not pretty, I must share

My head was in shackles
Which needed to go
Caught in the patterns
Like a curse of Saturn

The thoughts were like a broken record
Not in tune, or even rhyme

My words dousing my intuition
My listening causing more confusion

My brain pretending as if it knew
All the answers it had were true

By such habits I was caught
It had come to an impasse
Everything was shattering like a glass

The dream was now clear
For the new me to emerge
The old one had to disappear

Madame, you must die
So that I can live
As one with mind, body, emotions, spirit and thought!

Acceptance

Not always, things will happen my way. I will start the day with right intention to be happy and productive. Sometimes, life has other plans for me. Acceptance comes in handy, provided I keep it on the horizon.

The Ringing In My Ears

The ringing in my ears
Like all the signals got mixed up
Or like thousand bumble bees
Each buzzing a different song

You drive me nuts
The ringing in my ears

I know you won't go away
You are here to stay

I forget you during the day
At night, you make hay

Since you are here and I am here
Every single day of the year

Come, let's play
You a song-bird singing different songs
I a bird-lover in awe of your talent, all year long

Duality Of Life

The days are separate
Yet life is one
Every day is new
Yet brings the old
I wake up to a fresh morning
But bring the stale night with it
How to separate the two
Yet let them flow into each other
This is the duality of life

Who Shall Write?

Daring ones dare
It is an overcast day
I am by the mountain
In my hotel room
At Blackcomb ski resort

The daring ones are up
On the mountain with their skis
And they come zig zagging down
They get the thrill
Again, they go up the hill
The rain comes pouring down
The daring ones stay
For one more ride
Then two, three and four

I sip my tea
They dare
In the whitest of the white
Otherwise, who shall write?

Simplicity

The charm today
Is in its simplicity
Its expectedness
Its routine
In the meditation
The sameness
Sometimes you don't need a lot
A little will suffice

A Gorgeous Autumn Morning

My energy slowly coming back
The yellow and golden leaves cover the ground
Create a soft and inviting path
I slowly step on it
I walk on it
It cushions me
Life is changing every second
Love is accepting
Reassuring

Can My Soul Be Free?

Free when I am bound
Free when I am stuck
Free when life feels like a drag
Free when I feel like I hog

Can my soul be free?

Free when I fear failure
Free when I am a pawn to the past
Free when I am anxious of the future
Free when I fear others
Free when I fear for others

Can my soul be free?

Free to feel the wind
Free to float in the clouds
Free to sense the joy
Free to accept life just as is
Can my soul be free?

Anu Arora

Letting Go

I wonder
I wonder

What should I let go?
What must I remove?
So that I allow
New to come in
And manifest

I wonder
I wonder
Is it attachment or doubt?
Or is it insecurity which holds me back?
Or is it, that I don't know
What I don't know

What should I let go?

Surrender

The silence of a pause is:
Deafening
The surrender to the unknown:
Frightening
All the logic of the world is:
Fighting
Yet surrender is the only way

To the cosmic and mystical universe
I surrender to thee

Strange Feeling

Have you ever felt?
An extreme sorrow and joy
At the same moment
It is hard to tell,
If the tears running down my cheeks
Are of happiness or despair

Have you ever felt?
Relieved and burdened
By the same weight
Weight lifting off and becoming heavy
At the exact moment

It is a strange feeling
The universe is creating
Space for me
To free my soul

It feels uncomfortable
It is painful

Through discomfort, comes the change
It will open the space
For my soul to be free

I Live To Die

I live to die
A death of a yogi

When the moment is near
And the whole life flashes in front of me

I can smile
For I lived every day as if it was the first
With curiosity and a childlike innocence

For I lived every day as if it was my last
Counting my blessings
Warming others hearts

My time on earth was worthwhile

My body strong
My heart still warm

In a nano second
My soul was gone

I must live like a yogi
If I want to die like one

The Discovery Zone

For the last few weeks
I was suspended
In the discovery zone

It was magical
As I was transforming
From caterpillar to butterfly
From being on earth to learning to fly
In color, grace and beauty
Which can't even be described
I was mesmerized

It was painful
The decayed, gangrene infected
Body parts, which couldn't be saved
I had to let go of them
And everything, I was holding on to

Being in the discovery zone was not easy
Not being there was painful too

The pain will go, the wounds will heal
A new me will explore the world in
A different kind of way

I won't have known this life
Had I not gone into the discovery zone

Celebration

Life is a celebration. Some days there is a set reason. On other days, we have to find one. My desire is to make every day of my life a celebration. Some days turn into beautiful ones as a result.

Happy New Year With A Slight Backward Bend

With feet firmly connected
to mother Earth
in surrender to the reality

With the lift coming from the
bottom of the belly,
to the heart,
to the crown of my head
in aspiration for the year to come

With hands folded in prayer
to the universe
for positivity, love and health for everyone

With a slight backbend
to acknowledge the year gone
Yes, you were good
And there were experiences gained
Lessons learnt

It is time to move ahead
Happy New Year
I am curious
What new we will create with each other

Every Day Is A Gift

I celebrate my life
For its breath
I celebrate my life
For its quest
I celebrate my life
For my heart can sing
I celebrate my life
For the gifts it brings
I am blessed to the core
And I am being showered with more
With gratitude, I soak all in
Every day is a gift

The River Flows Again

It flows again
Slowly, a bit hesitant
Like it's on the training wheels
Forgot how effortlessly it did, not so long ago

It got some rain
It can breathe again
Back to its true nature
It smiles again

Out of balance, I had seen
Day after day of scorching sun
Still and sluggish
All dried up, unable to move
Contaminated by algae and more

The birds didn't rest
The humans didn't canoe
As it lay there listless and lifeless

Back to balance and in agony no more
The river has started to flow again

Celebrations

Every flower in a vase
Every vase full of flowers
The entire bloom of the town
Has filled every corner of my house

It is momentary
It will be gone

But, it is the moment I have lived
It is the nectar I have sipped
I have flown to moon and back
Never before I could claim that

I dared an impossible dream
I met the sun at its very high
I caressed the stars shining bright
I trembled at my own strength
The transition to reality in front of my eyes

And when the candle did I blow
I felt all those tears flow
A tear for the moment lived
A tear for the nectar sipped
A tear for the love around

For you don't live your dreams alone
A tear for everyone who lived my dream
I am sure what will not be gone
The little bit of myself I have found!

I also know that there is more to know
For that I need to sow!

Happy Mother's Day, Mom

Today during a long bike ride
I talked about you
Just about you

Your beauty, grace and your charm
Your undying affection for your loved ones
Asking little in return

Standing tall and dignified during adversities
You got plenty of them for a lifetime
Encouraging, motivating and uplifting for others
When your own heart was bleeding

Doing the best at everything you tried your hands on
An agriculturalist, a baker, a badminton player and a cook
I always knew when you made my favorite dishes
The scent traveled to my school

I shared my teenage crushes with you
I shared my silly jokes with you
I shared my medals/prizes with you

You laughed, chuckled, and your heart swelled with pride
I held your hand and said, 'Don't ever leave me, mom. I
will need you every step of the way.'

And you said, 'I will be there with you, always there
for you.'
I feel your presence, mom
I feel your joy, I feel your light
My guardian angel, my guiding force
Always shining incredibly bright

Happy Mother's Day, Mom

ABOUT ANU ARORA

Anu Arora is the founder of Infinite Potential Leadership. Her company explores opportunities and ways to expand human potential to the infinite. They are the creator, leader and facilitators of 'Ignite your light' programs, training individuals, government and corporations in becoming wholistic, productive and far-reaching in their impact.

Her company specializes in leadership and executive coaching, happiness and mindfulness trainings.

You can find more about her and her company at www.infinitepotentialleadership.com

Anu Arora

ABOUT 'IGNITE YOUR LIGHT' PROGRAMS

'Ignite Your Light' are one of the kind workshops and retreats designed to help you explore your infinite potential. There are many areas of exploration that make the whole 'YOU'. The programs focus on proven and effective tools and techniques which you get to practice as a part of the program.

Subscribe at www.infinitepotentialleadership.com to get the latest news and information about these programs.

Made in the USA
Coppell, TX
26 January 2022

72384239R00062